EMERALD CATHEDRAL

Inside a Tropical Rain Forest

by Gregory Marks

HOUGHTON MIFFLIN BOSTON

The first recorded description of a New World tropical rain forest came from its first European tourist, Christopher Columbus. "Never [have I] beheld so fair a thing," he wrote. After learning that he did not land in the East Indies, he decided he had found the Garden of Eden.

More than ten years later, in what is now Brazil, explorer Amerigo Vespucci said of the rain forest, "If Paradise could be found anywhere on Earth, it wouldn't be far from [this] country!"

This tropical rain forest lines the coastline of Costa Rica's Manuel Antonio National Park.

Tropical Rain Forests

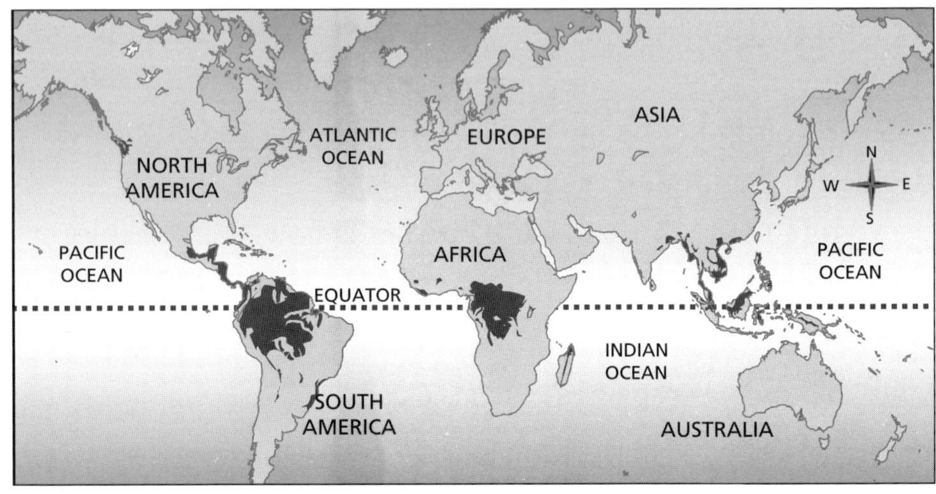

No wonder the explorers admired these forests. What brilliant color! What breathtaking beauty! Such forests can exist only in the tropics—two bands extending about 1500 miles north and south of the equator. Rain forests in other zones are different from tropical forests.

Tropical rain forests cover only seven percent of the Earth's land surface. But they are home to fifty percent of its plants and animals.

Why are tropical rain forests so rich with life? In the tropics, temperatures change very little throughout the year. Rain forests are always hot and wet. The air is often humid. Year round, the sun's direct rays keep average daily temperatures between 73 and 87 degrees.

These warm, wet forests give life to more than 30 million species of plants and animals. Many are still unknown to scientists. Broad leaves cover the trees year round. Plants flower and fruit throughout the year. They feed millions of animals.

A Layered Forest

Early explorers could not see the most enchanting parts of the forest. From the ground, a dense mass of leaves, branches, and vines hides the life that bustles and blooms in the treetops.

Rain forests form separate layers that are quite different from one another. Some animals move from layer to layer. Some plants reach from one layer into another. Many plants and animals never leave the layer they occupy. But their lives are linked with organisms in other layers that they never see.

Emergents: Tallest trees that stretch 75–250 feet from the floor

Canopy: Roof-like layer formed by spreading branches of treetops 40–75 feet from floor

Understory: Layer of tall shrubs and shorter trees extending 40 feet from floor

Floor: ground level

The Forest Floor

Visitors have compared the forest floor to a giant emerald cathedral. Trees tower like columns, disappearing into an arching canopy. Chatter, squawks, and shrieks break the warm, humid stillness. These sounds hint at the life that teems above.

Only slivers of light slip through the dense plant growth. Few green plants grow in the dim shadows of the lowest layer. They include ferns, baby trees, and shrubs that can live with little light. Members of the ginger family grow here. Some mosses and fungi feed on nutrients in the trunks and roots of tall trees.

The floor seems hushed and still. But the heavy scent of life fills the air. Animals lurk in the shadows. Some bustle unseen beneath the carpet of leaves and twigs. Ground animals hunt for fallen fruits and nuts.

Floor animals act as gardeners. They scatter and fertilize the seeds of fruit-bearing trees. They eat the fruit. Then they drop the seeds in a pile of nutrient-rich dung some distance from the parent tree. Trees and plants take root. Some animals even plant the seeds.

The floor depends on the upper forest for nutrients and gives back nutrients to the towering trees. Millions of insects and tiny organisms eat fallen leaves, branches, fruit, and animal droppings. They break them down into nutrients for the trees and plants.

Floor Animals and Hunters

Floor-walking birds, such as the banded pitta, eat insects. Larger mammals, such as the anteater, also feed on insects. At night, its relative, the armadillo, takes a turn eating insects.

The long snout and sticky tongue of the anteater are perfect for dining in ant and termite mounds.

Insects also feed frogs and toads. The forest floor is so damp that frogs can live and lay their eggs on it.

In turn, plant- and insect-eating animals become meals for prowling predators. The bird-eating spider hunts for frogs, lizards, small rodents, small birds, and bats.

The bird-eating spider is the world's largest. Like a cat, this tarantula sneaks up on its prey and pounces. This fear-some hunter can also be prey. Some South Americans enjoy tarantulas roasted over a campfire.

The largest predator in the Brazilian rain forest is the jaguar. To find enough food, one jaguar must range over as many as 200 square miles. A swimmer and climber, it hunts in the water, in the trees, and on the floor. On the floor, it hunts such animals as deer, pig-like animals called peccaries, tapirs, and the capybara.

The jaguar has little need to fear other animals, unless it startles a poisonous snake. The deadly fer de lance, pit viper, or night-prowling bushmaster may be coiled on the forest floor.

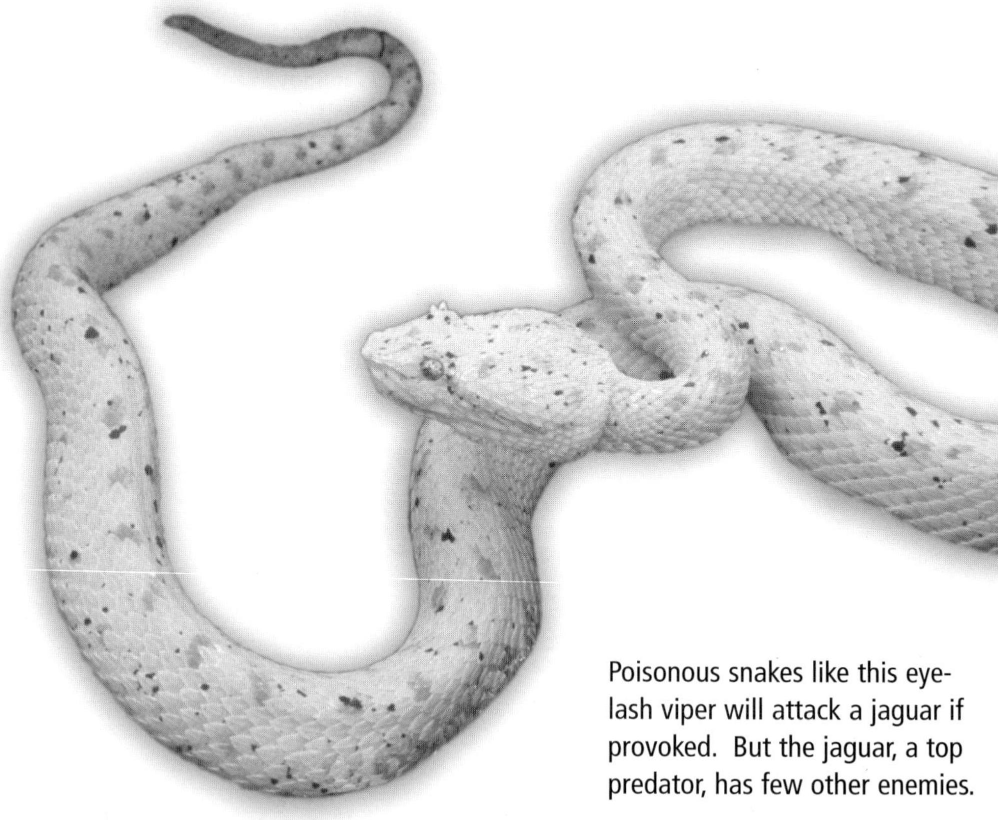

Poisonous snakes like this eyelash viper will attack a jaguar if provoked. But the jaguar, a top predator, has few other enemies.

Some animals on the forest floor are visitors from upper layers. They may even carry passengers, as does the three-toed sloth. The sloth spends its life in the trees, eating leaves or hanging motionless under branches. Covered with green algae, it blends in with the forest leaves. Its fur is home to insects that can survive only in sloth fur, such as sloth moths and some beetles and mites.

Once a week, the sloth climbs down to use its bathroom—the forest floor. Beetles and moths jump off to lay eggs in its waste. Moths hatching from the last visit jump into the sloth's fur for the ride up.

The female sloth is always carrying a baby, inside or out. As soon as one baby sloth stops clinging, the mother becomes pregnant again.

The understory is the home of the chocolate-producing cacao tree. Like many understory trees, the cacao grows fruits and flowers directly out of its trunk.

The Understory

The branches above the understory block most of the sunlight and hold moisture in the air. In the dim, greenish light, the shrubs and young trees rarely grow tall. Palms, ancient cone-bearing trees, ferns, and delicate shade-loving plants enjoy this humid layer.

Understory plants grow leaves broad enough to gather the limited sunlight. Many leaf-eating insects, reptiles, and mammals prefer feeding or nesting in this layer. Iguanas—lizard-like reptiles as long as six feet—sometimes munch on understory leaves. Insect-eating birds and tree frogs also dine well.

The ocelot prowls the understory, preying on unsuspecting leaf-eaters.

These leaf and insect eaters attract predators to the understory. Small cats called ocelots and marguys lie in wait. Palm vipers, poisonous snakes that eat birds and look like branches, may lurk in understory trees. Also camouflaged in the understory are boa constrictors and anacondas, climbing snakes that can hunt on any level.

THE CANOPY

Most plant growth takes place in the canopy. Here, a network of flowering vines joins the spreading crowns of treetops. Plants bask in a sunlit paradise.

In the canopy, the forest explodes into color and life. Flowers, birds, and butterflies flash blue, yellow, and red against green leaves.

Colorful parrots, macaws, and many species of hummingbirds fly through the canopy. About half of all American songbirds winter in the tropical rain forest.

The brightly colored bill of the toucan is so large that it looks as if this bird stuck its head in a huge crab claw.

Canopy flowers depend on insects, birds, and bats to carry their pollen. Some flowers, such as certain orchids, can be pollinated by only one species of animal. Each plant makes flowers to attract the animals that pollinate it. Birds like brightly colored flowers. Bees are attracted to flowers partly by smell and partly by lively colors. Plants that depend on bats have white flowers with powerful smells to help night flyers find them in the dark.

The orchid bee, part of an interdependent process, pollinates the flowers of Brazil nut trees.

Forest organisms can form partnerships among two, three, and even four or five elements. Partners may live on levels from the floor to the canopy. For example, many South Americans earn money gathering nuts from the Brazil nut tree. The tree depends on the agouti to free and plant its seeds. It also needs partners in the canopy to pollinate it. Only a strong bee such as an orchid bee can pollinate its flowers. Orchid bees cannot reproduce without certain substances from orchids. If orchid bees, orchids, or agoutis disappear in an area, so will the Brazil nut trees. People who collect their nuts will lose their income.

Many rain forest plants occupy three layers, from their roots on the floor to their flowers in the canopy. Some plants depend on tall trees to boost them up to the sunlight. Vines climb trunks from the floor to the canopy seeking sunlight.

Some flowering plants, such as orchids, do not have roots in the ground. They live only on high canopy branches. Their roots and leaves take food from sunlight, rainwater, dust, and animal droppings. These plants produce flowers of breathtaking beauty. The large flowers of one such plant family, the bromeliads, have cupped centers that hold water.

Animals drink from the cupped centers of bromeliad flowers that hold up to two gallons of water. Insects and frogs make homes in these cups. Their waste products supply nutrients to the plant.

Millions of canopy animals feast on the garden of fruits, seeds, leaves, and nuts. The wealth of canopy plants supports most of the rain forest animals. Many of these species, such as monkeys, move easily from tree to tree on a network of branches and vines.

Plants depend on canopy animals to carry seeds a distance from the parent tree. At any given time, only some trees will be fruiting, and may be widely scattered. Some animals, such as the golden lion tamarin, need to range over a large expanse of canopy to find enough food. They may disappear if the forest is broken up into small patches.

Monkeys are wasteful eaters, dropping seeds that take root and bits of fruit for floor animals to enjoy. These howler monkeys are known for loud wails that warn other howlers away from their home ranges.

On the ground or in the canopy, the poison dart frog is protected by a strong poison in its skin. Some South American Indians hunt the frog for its poison, which they apply to the tips of darts shot from blowguns.

Many animals spend their entire lives in the canopy, feasting on the food it provides. They drink from leaves and the cupped centers of flowers. Others visit the ground at times.

For example, the brightly colored poison dart frog lives in trees. But the female lays eggs on the floor. When the tadpoles hatch, she carries them up to live in their tree homes.

The Emergent Layer

Other animals visit the canopy only to hunt. Birds of prey, such as the harpy eagle, nest high in majestic trees that extend above the canopy. Here, crowns of giant trees spread like open umbrellas to form the emergent layer. At this height, strong tropical winds can whip the treetops. Many insects live in this layer. But most of the flowers are pollinated by wind.

Birds of prey nest high in emergent trees, where they can spot small animals in the canopy and swoop down on them.

To preserve the rain forest, Indians who live there hunt or harvest its products without clearing the land. Above, a Matses woman weaves a basket from palm leaves in a rain forest near Angamos, in the Amazon Basin, Peru.

Bad News: The Falling Forest

Tropical rain forests are shrinking. According to some scientists, as many as 27,000 rain forest species may vanish every year as forests are cut down around the world.

The Brazilian Atlantic rain forest began to fall in the early 1500s when settlers devoured it chunk by chunk. Logging and clearing forests provided homes, food, fuel, money, and jobs. But Indians lost their way of life, as well as their means of survival. So did many plants and animals. Many toppled trees were hundreds or thousands of years old. A way of life was becoming extinct.

Even in the remaining patches, many species are at risk. Some species live only in one small rain forest community. If their home is cleared, such species are gone forever. Other species need large ranges to find food or mates. They cannot survive when cleared areas break the forest into small sections.

Many shade plants and organisms cannot grow outside their shadowy habitat. Patches of forest cannot reseed and fertilize the large cleared area. Without a standing forest to drop nutrients, rain forest soils are poor.

The diversity of a cleared forest may never be replaced. Rain forest communities have evolved over millions of years. Once the web is broken, plants and animals cannot rebuild their complex communities.

Cleared rain forest land makes poor farmland. Once the soil is worn out, it loses the network of plants and roots that hold it in place. Then the bare soil is quickly washed away by heavy tropical storms.

In all ecosystems, plants and animals depend on one another. Extinction of one species may put others at risk.

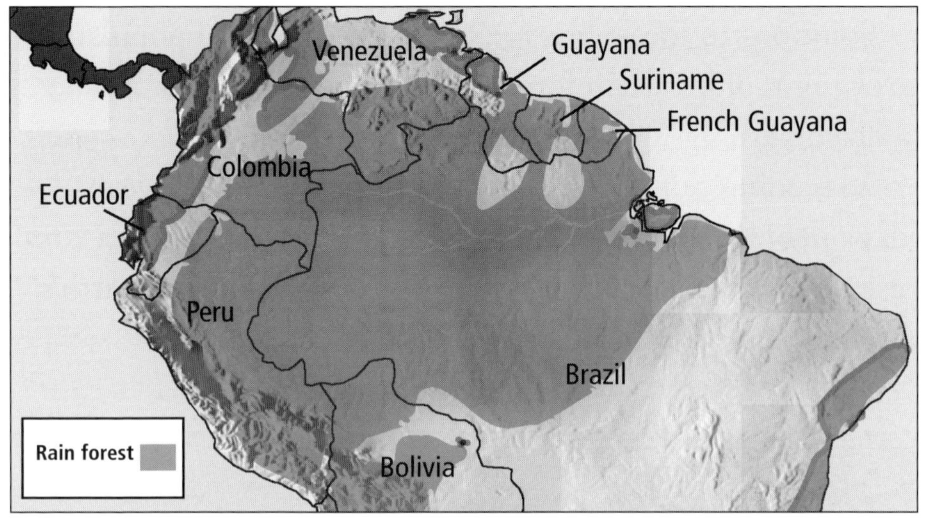

Good News: The Remaining Forest

The good news is that two million square miles of Amazon rain forest still sprawl across the Amazon basin. The forest extends from Brazil into seven other countries.

To the Rescue

In Brazil and abroad, people, groups, and governments are trying to save the remaining rain forest. Areas have been set aside for natives to harvest fruits, nuts, and other products without cutting trees. For example, Brazil nuts and medicine plants are taken from rain forests without destroying them. Rubber and cacao can be collected from rain forest trees instead of being farmed. To help, rain forest groups have asked people to buy products gathered from standing forests.

Solutions to forest loss are not simple. World population is growing rapidly. Rain forest countries need to earn money and do something for their poor.

A standing rain forest can earn money year after year. Today's people must meet their needs in ways that preserve the forest. Perhaps then future generations can enjoy the Earth's richest and most beautiful ecosystem.

Buying harvested rain forest products creates a market for them. This market supports the native people's economy and way of life. Using these goods could make saving the rain forest more profitable than cutting it down.